HOW TO CHOOSE
A LEADERSHIP
PATTERN

Harvard Business Review

CLASSICS

HOW TO CHOOSE A LEADERSHIP PATTERN

Robert Tannenbaum and
Warren H. Schmidt

Harvard Business Press
Boston, Massachusetts

Copyright 2008 Harvard Business School Publishing Corporation

Originally published in the *Harvard Business Review* in 1973

Reprint #73311

All rights reserved

Printed in the United States of America

13 12 11 10 09   5 4 3 2 1

No part of this publication may be reproduced, stored in or introduced into a retrieval system, or transmitted, in any form, or by any means (electronic, mechanical, photocopying, recording, or otherwise), without the prior permission of the publisher. Requests for permission should be directed to permissions@hbsp.harvard.edu, or mailed to Permissions, Harvard Business School Publishing, 60 Harvard Way, Boston, Massachusetts 02163.

Library of Congress Cataloging-in-Publication Data
Tannenbaum, Robert.
  How to choose a leadership pattern / Robert Tannenbaum, Warren H. Schmidt.
    p. cm. – (The Harvard business review classics series)
    ISBN 978-1-4221-7552-1 (pbk. : alk. paper)
 1. Leadership. 2. Decision making. I. Schmidt, Warren H. II. Title.
  HD57.7.T367 2009
  658.4'092–dc22

2009010519

The paper used in this publication meets the requirements of the American National Standard for Permanence of Paper for Publications and Documents in Libraries and Archives Z39.48-1992.

THE HARVARD BUSINESS REVIEW CLASSICS SERIES

Since 1922, *Harvard Business Review* has been a leading source of breakthrough ideas in management practice—many of which still speak to and influence us today. The HBR Classics series now offers you the opportunity to make these seminal pieces a part of your permanent management library. Each volume contains a groundbreaking idea that has shaped best practices and inspired countless managers around the world—and will change how you think about the business world today.

HOW TO CHOOSE A LEADERSHIP PATTERN

"I put most problems into my group's hands and leave it to them to carry the ball from there. I serve merely as a catalyst, mirroring back the people's thoughts and feelings so that they can better understand them."

"It's foolish to make decisions oneself on matters that affect people. I always talk things over with my subordinates, but I make it clear to them that I'm the one who has to have the final say."

"Once I have decided on a course of action, I do my best to sell my ideas to my employees."

"I'm being paid to lead. If I let a lot of other people make the decisions I should be making, then I'm not worth my salt."

"I believe in getting things done. I can't waste time calling meetings. Someone has to call the shots around here, and I think it should be me."

Each of these statements represents a point of view about "good leadership." Considerable experience, factual data, and theoretical principles could be cited to support each statement, even though they seem to be inconsistent when placed together. Such contradictions point up the dilemma in

How to Choose a Leadership Pattern

which modern managers frequently find themselves.

NEW PROBLEM

The problem of how modern managers can be "democratic" in their relations with subordinates and at the same time maintain the necessary authority and control in the organizations for which they are responsible has come into focus increasingly in recent years.

Earlier in the century this problem was not so acutely felt. The successful executive was generally pictured as possessing intelligence, imagination, initiative, the capacity to make rapid (and generally wise) decisions, and the ability to inspire subordinates. People tended to think of the world as being divided into "leaders" and "followers."

New Focus

Gradually, however, from the social sciences emerged the concept of "group dynamics" with its focus on *members* of the group rather than solely on the leader. Research efforts of social scientists underscored the importance of employee involvement and participation in decision making. Evidence began to challenge the efficiency of highly directive leadership, and increasing attention was paid to problems of motivation and human relations.

Through training laboratories in group development that sprang up across the

How to Choose a Leadership Pattern

country, many of the newer notions of leadership began to exert an impact. These training laboratories were carefully designed to give people a firsthand experience in full participation and decision making. The designated "leaders" deliberately attempted to reduce their own power and to make group members as responsible as possible for setting their own goals and methods within the laboratory experience.

It was perhaps inevitable that some of the people who attended the training laboratories regarded this kind of leadership as being truly "democratic" and went home with the determination to build fully participative deison making into their own organizations. Whenever their bosses made a decision without convening a staff meeting, they tended to perceive this as authoritarian behavior. The true symbol of democratic leadership to some was the meeting—and the less directed from the top, the more democratic it was.

Some of the more enthusiastic alumni of these training laboratories began to get the habit of categorizing leader behavior as "democratic" *or* "authoritarian." Bosses who made too many decisions themselves were thought of as authoritarian, and their directive behavior was often attributed solely to their personalities.

New Need

The net result of the research findings and of the human relations training based

How to Choose a Leadership Pattern

upon them has been to call into question the stereotype of an effective leader. Consequently, modern managers often find themselves in an uncomfortable state of mind.

Often they are not quite sure how to behave; there are times when they are torn between exerting "strong" leadership and "permissive" leadership. Sometimes new knowledge pushes them in one direction ("I should really get the group to help make this decision"), but at the same time their experience pushes them in another direction ("I really understand the problem better than the group and therefore I should make the decision"). They are not sure when a group decision is really appropriate or when holding a staff meeting serves merely as a device for avoiding their own decision-making responsibility.

The purpose of our article is to suggest a framework which managers may find useful in grappling with this dilemma. First, we shall look at the different patterns of leadership behavior that managers can choose from in relating to their subordinates. Then, we shall turn to some of the questions suggested by this range of patterns. For instance, how important is it for managers' subordinates to know what type of leadership they are using in a situation? What factors should they consider in deciding on a leadership pattern? What difference do their long-run objectives make as compared to their immediate objectives?

How to Choose a Leadership Pattern

RANGE OF BEHAVIOR

Exhibit I presents the continuum or range of possible leadership behavior available to managers. Each type of action is related to the degree of authority used by the boss and to the amount of freedom available to subordinates in reaching decisions. The actions seen on the extreme left characterize managers who maintain a high degree of control while those seen on the extreme right characterize managers who release a high degree of control. Neither extreme is absolute; authority and freedom are never without their limitations.

Now let us look more closely at each of the behavior points occurring along this continuum.

EXHIBIT 1

Continuum of leadership behavior

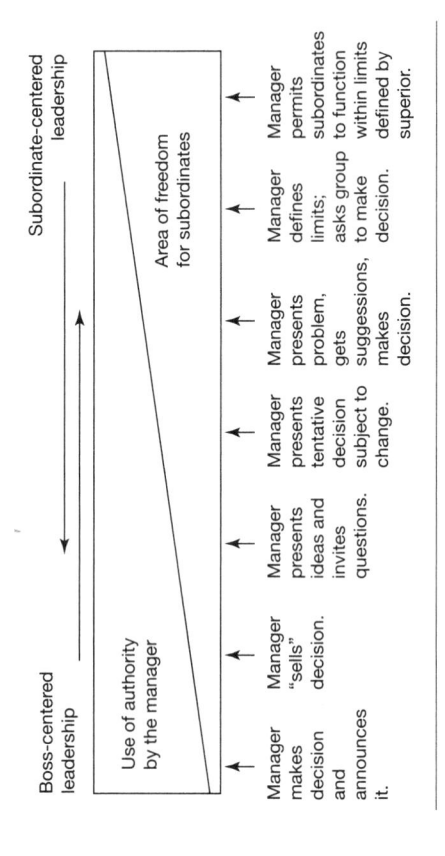

Boss-centered leadership ←——————————————→ Subordinate-centered leadership

Use of authority by the manager

Area of freedom for subordinates

- Manager makes decision and announces it.
- Manager "sells" decision.
- Manager presents ideas and invites questions.
- Manager presents tentative decision subject to change.
- Manager presents problem, gets suggestions, makes decision.
- Manager defines limits; asks group to make decision.
- Manager permits subordinates to function within limits defined by superior.

How to Choose a Leadership Pattern

The manager makes the decision and announces it

In this case the boss identifies a problem, considers alternative solutions, chooses one of them, and then reports this decision to the subordinates for implementation. The boss may or may not give consideration to what he or she believes the subordinates will think or feel about the decision; in any case, no opportunity is provided for them to participate directly in the decision-making process. Coercion may or may not be used or implied.

The manager "sells" the decision

Here the manager, as before, takes responsibility for identifying the problem and arriving at a decision. However, rather than simply announcing it, he or she takes the additional step of persuading the subordinates to accept it. In doing so, the boss recognizes the possibility of some resistance among those who will be faced with the decision, and seeks to reduce this resistance by indicating, for example, what the employees have to gain from the decision.

The manager presents ideas, invites questions

Here the boss who has arrived at a decision and who seeks acceptance of his or her ideas provides an opportunity for subordinates to get a fuller explanation of his or her thinking and intentions. After presenting the ideas, the manager invites questions so that the associates can better understand what he or she is trying to accomplish. This "give and take" also enables the manager and the subordinates to explore more fully the implications of the decision.

The manager presents a tentative decision subject to change

This kind of behavior permits the subordinates to exert some influence on the decision. The initiative for identifying and diagnosing the problem remains with the boss. Before meeting with the staff, the manager has thought the problem through and arrived at a decision—but only a tentative one. Before finalizing it, he or she presents the proposed solution for the reaction of those who will be affected by it. He or she says in effect, "I'd like to hear what you have to say about this plan that I have developed. I'll appreciate your frank reactions but will reserve for myself the final decision."

The manager presents the problem, gets suggestions, and then makes the decision

Up to this point the boss has come before the group with a solution of his or her own. Not so in this case. The subordinates now get the first chance to suggest solutions. The manager's initial role involves identifying the problem. He or she might, for example, say something of this sort: "We are faced with a number of complaints from newspapers and the general public on our service policy.

How to Choose a Leadership Pattern

What is wrong here? What ideas do you have for coming to grips with this problem?"

The function of the group becomes one of increasing the manager's repertory of possible solutions to the problem. The purpose is to capitalize on the knowledge and experience of those who are on the "firing line." From the expanded list of alternatives developed by the manager and the subordinates, the manager then selects the solution that he or she regards as most promising.[1]

The manager defines the limits and requests the group to make a decision

At this point the manager passes to the group (possibly taking part as a member) the right to make decisions. Before doing so, however, he or she defines the problem to be solved and the boundaries within which the decision must be made.

An example might be the handling of a parking problem at a plant. The boss decides that this is something that should be worked on by the people involved, so they are called together. Pointing up the existence of the problem, the boss tells them:

> There is the open field just north of the main plant which has been designated for additional employee parking. We can build underground or surface multilevel facilities as long as the cost does not exceed $100,000. Within these limits we are free to work out whatever solution makes sense to us. After we decide on a specific plan, the company will spend the available money in whatever way we indicate.

How to Choose a Leadership Pattern

The manager permits the group to make decisions within prescribed limits

This represents an extreme degree of group freedom only occasionally encountered in formal organizations, as, for instance, in many research groups. Here the team of managers or engineers undertakes the identification and diagnosis of the problem, develops alternative procedures for solving it, and decides on one or more of these alternative solutions. The only limits directly imposed on the group by the organization are those specified by the superior of the team's boss. If the boss participates in the decision-making process, deciding in advance to assist in implementing whatever decision the group makes, he or she attempts to do so with no more authority than any other member of the group.

KEY QUESTIONS

As the continuum in Exhibit I demonstrates, there are a number of alternative ways in which managers can relate themselves to the group or individuals they are supervising. At the extreme left of the range, the emphasis is on the manager—on what *he* or *she* is interested in, how *he* or *she* sees things, how *he* or *she* feels about them. As we move toward the subordinate-centered end of the continuum, however, the focus is increasingly on the subordinates— on what *they* are interested in, how *they* look at things, how *they* feel about them.

How to Choose a Leadership Pattern

When business leadership is regarded in this way, a number of questions arise. Let us take four of especial importance.

Can bosses ever relinquish their responsibility by delegating it to others?

Our view is that managers must expect to be held responsible by their superiors for the quality of the decisions made, even though operationally these decisions may have been made on a group basis. They should, therefore, be ready to accept whatever risk is involved whenever they delegate decision-making power to subordinates. Delegation is not a way of "passing the buck." Also, it should be emphasized that the amount of freedom bosses give to subordinates cannot be greater than the freedom which they themselves have been given by their own superiors.

Should the manager participate with subordinates once he or she has delegated responsibility to them?

Managers should carefully think over this question and decide on their role prior to involving the subordinate group. They should ask if their presence will inhibit or failitate the problem-solving process. There may be some instances when they should leave the group to let it solve the problem for itself. Typically, however, the boss has useful ideas to contribute and should function as an additional member of the group. In the latter instance, it is important that he or she indicate clearly to the group that he or she is in a member role rather than an authority role.

How important is it for the group to recognize what kind of leadership behavior the boss is using?

It makes a great deal of difference. Many relationship problems between bosses and subordinates occur because the bosses fail to make clear how they plan to use their authority. If, for example, the boss actually intends to make a certain decision, but the subordinate group gets the impression that he or she has delegated this authority, considerable confusion and resentment are likely to follow. Problems may also occur when the boss uses a "democratic" facade to conceal the fact that he or she has already made a decision which he or she hopes the group will accept as its own. The attempt to "make them think it was their idea in the first place" is a risky one. We believe that it is highly important for managers to be honest and clear in describing what authority they are keeping and what role they are asking their subordinates to assume in solving a particular problem.

Can you tell how "democratic" a manager is by the number of decisions the subordinates make?

The sheer *number* of decisions is not an accurate index of the amount of freedom that a subordinate group enjoys. More important is the *significance* of the decisions which the boss entrusts to subordinates. Obviously a decision on how to arrange desks is of an entirely different order from a decision involving the introduction of new electronic data-processing equipment. Even though the widest possible limits are given in dealing with the first issue, the group will sense no particular degree of responsibility. For a boss to permit the group to decide equipment policy, even within rather narrow limits, would reflect a greater degree of confidence in them on his or her part.

DECIDING HOW TO LEAD

Now let us turn from the types of leadership which are possible in a company situation to the question of what types are *practical* and *desirable*. What factors or forces should a manager consider in deciding how to manage? Three are of particular importance:

- Forces in the manager.
- Forces in the subordinates.
- Forces in the situation.

We should like briefly to describe these elements and indicate how they might influence a manager's action in a decision-making situation.[2] The strength of each of them will, of course, vary from instance to instance, but managers who are sensitive to them can better assess the problems which face them and determine which mode of

How to Choose a Leadership Pattern

leadership behavior is most appropriate for them.

Forces in the Manager

The manager's behavior in any given instance will be influenced greatly by the many forces operating within his or her own personality. Managers will, of course, perceive their leadership problems in a unique way on the basis of their background, knowledge, and experience. Among the important internal forces affecting them will be the following:

1. *Their value system.* How strongly do they feel that individuals should have a share in making the decisions which

affect them? Or, how convinced are they that the official who is paid to assume responsibility should personally carry the burden of decision making? The strength of their convictions on questions like these will tend to move managers to one end or the other of the continuum shown in Exhibit I. Their behavior will also be influenced by the relative importance that they attach to organizational efficiency, personal growth of subordinates, and company profits.[3]

2. *Their confidence in subordinates.* Managers differ greatly in the amount of trust they have in other people

How to Choose a Leadership Pattern

generally, and this carries over to the particular employees they supervise at a given time. In viewing his or her particular group of subordinates, the manager is likely to consider their knowledge and competence with respect to the problem. A central question managers might ask themselves is: "Who is best qualified to deal with this problem?" Often they may, justifiably or not, have more confidence in their own capabilities than in those of subordinates.

3. *Their own leadership inclinations.* There are some managers who seem to function more comfortably and

naturally as highly directive leaders. Resolving problems and issuing orders come easily to them. Other managers seem to operate more comfortably in a team role, where they are continually sharing many of their functions with their subordinates.

4. *Their feelings of security in an uncertain situation.* Managers who release control over the decision-making process thereby reduce the predictability of the outcome. Some managers have a greater need than others for predictability and stability in their environment. This "tolerance for ambiguity" is being viewed

increasingly by psychologists as a key variable in a person's manner of dealing with problems.

Managers bring these and other highly personal variables to each situation they face. If they can see them as forces which, consciously or unconsciously, influence their behavior, they can better understand what makes them prefer to act in a given way. And understanding this, they can often make themselves more effective.

Forces in the Subordinate

Before deciding how to lead a certain group, managers will also want to consider a number of forces affecting their subordinates' behavior. They will want to remember that each employee, like themselves, is influenced by many personality variables. In addition, each subordinate has a set of expectations about how the boss should act in relation to him or her (the phrase "expected behavior" is one we hear more and more often these days at discussions of leadership and teaching). The better managers understand these factors, the more accurately they can determine what kind of behavior on their part will enable subordinates to act most effectively.

Generally speaking, managers can permit subordinates greater freedom if the following essential conditions exist:

- If the subordinates have relatively high needs for independence. (As we all know, people differ greatly in the amount of direction that they desire.)

- If the subordinates have a readiness to assume responsibility for decision making. (Some see additional responsibility as a tribute to their ability; others see it as "passing the buck.")

- If they have a relatively high tolerance for ambiguity. (Some employees prefer to have clear-cut directives given to them; others prefer a wider area of freedom.)

- If they are interested in the problem and feel that it is important.

- If they understand and identify with the goals of the organization.

- If they have the necessary knowledge and experience to deal with the problem.

- If they have learned to expect to share in decision making. (Persons who have come to expect strong leadership and are then suddenly confronted with the request to share more fully in decision making are often upset by this new experience. On the other hand, persons who have enjoyed a considerable amount of freedom resent bosses who begin to make all the decisions themselves.)

Managers will probably tend to make fuller use of their own authority if the above conditions do *not* exist; at times there may be no realistic alternative to running a "one-man show."

The restrictive effect of many of the forces will, of course, be greatly modified by the general feeling of confidence which subordinates have in the boss. Where they have learned to respect and trust the boss, he or she is free to vary his or her own behavior. The boss will feel certain that he or she will not be perceived as an authoritarian boss on those occasions when he or she makes decisions alone. Similarly, the boss will not be seen as using staff meetings to avoid decision-making responsibility. In a climate of mutual confidence and respect, people tend to feel less threatened by deviations from normal practice, which in turn makes possible a higher degree of flexibility in the whole relationship.

Forces in the Situation

In addition to the forces which exist in managers themselves and in the subordinates, certain characteristics of the general situation will also affect managers' behavior. Among the more critical environmental pressures that surround them are those which stem from the organization, the work group, the nature of the problem, and the pressures of time. Let us look briefly at each of these:

Type of organization—Like individuals, organizations have values and traditions which inevitably influence the behavior of the people who work in them. Managers who are newcomers to a company quickly discover that certain kinds of behavior are approved while others are not. They also discover that to deviate radically from what is generally accepted is likely to create problems for them.

These values and traditions are communicated in numerous ways—through job descriptions, policy pronouncements, and public statements by top executives. Some organizations, for example, hold to the notion that the desirable executive is one who is dynamic, imaginative, decisive, and persuasive. Other organizations put more emphasis upon the importance of the executive's ability to work effectively with people—human relations skills. The fact that the person's superiors have a defined concept of what the good executive should be will very likely push the manager toward one end or the other of the behavioral range.

In addition to the above, the amount of employee participation is influenced by such variables as the size of the working units, their geographical distribution, and the degree of inter- and intra-organizational security required to attain company goals. For example, the wide geographical dispersion of an organization may preclude a practical system of participative decision making, even though this would otherwise be desirable. Similarly, the size of the working units or the need for keeping plans confidential may make it necessary for the boss to

How to Choose a Leadership Pattern

exercise more control than would otherwise be the case. Factors like these may limit considerably the manager's ability to function flexibly on the continuum.

Group effectiveness—Before turning decision-making responsibility over to a subordinate group, the boss should consider how effectively its members work together as a unit.

One of the relevant factors here is the experience the group has had in working together. It can generally be expected that a group which has functioned for some time will have developed habits of cooperation and thus be able to tackle a problem more effectively than a new group. It can also be expected that a group of people with similar backgrounds and interests will work more quickly and easily than people with dissimilar backgrounds, because the communication problems are likely to be less complex.

The degree of confidence that the members have in their ability to solve problems as a group is also a key consideration. Finally, such group variables as cohesiveness, permissiveness, mutual acceptance, and commonality of purpose will exert subtle but powerful influence on the group's functioning.

The problem itself—The nature of the problem may determine what degree of authority should be delegated by managers to their subordinates. Obviously, managers will ask themselves whether subordinates have the kind of knowledge which is needed. It is possible to do them a real disservice by assigning a problem that their experience does not equip them to handle.

Since the problems faced in large or growing industries increasingly require knowledge of specialists from many different fields, it might be inferred that the more complex a problem, the more anxious a manager will be to get some assistance in solving it. However, this is not always the case. There will be times when the very complexity of the problem calls for one person to work it out. For example, if the manager has most of the background and factual data relevant to a given issue, it may be easier for him or her to think it through than to take the time to fill in the staff on all the pertinent background information.

The key question to ask, of course, is: "Have I heard the ideas of everyone who has the necessary knowledge to make a significant contribution to the solution of this problem?"

The pressure of time–This is perhaps the most clearly felt pressure on managers (in spite of the fact that it may sometimes be imagined). The more that they feel the need for an immediate decision, the more difficult it is to involve other people. In organizations which are in a constant state of "crisis" and "crash programming" one is likely to find managers personally using a high degree of authority with relatively little delegation to subordinates. When the time pressure is less intense, however, it becomes much more

How to Choose a Leadership Pattern

possible to bring subordinates in on the decision-making process.

These, then, are the principal forces that impinge on managers in any given instance and that tend to determine their tactical behavior in relation to subordinates. In each case their behavior ideally will be that which makes possible the most effective attainment of their immediate goals within the limits facing them.

LONG-RUN STRATEGY

As managers work with their organizations on the problems that come up day to day, their choice of a leadership pattern is usually limited. They must take account of the forces just described and, within the restrictions those factors impose on them, do the best that they can. But as they look ahead months or even years, they can shift their thinking from tactics to large-scale strategy. No longer need they be fettered by all of the forces mentioned, for they can view many of them as variables over which they have some control. They can, for example, gain new insights or skills for themselves, supply training for individual subordinates, and provide participative experiences for their employee group.

In trying to bring about a change in these variables, however, they are faced with a challenging question: At which point along the continuum *should* they act?

Attaining objectives: The answer depends largely on what they want to accomplish. Let us suppose that they are interested in the same objectives that most modern managers seek to attain when they can shift their attention from the pressure of immediate assignments:

1. To raise the level of employee motivation.

2. To increase the readiness of subordinates to accept change.

3. To improve the quality of all managerial decisions.

4. To develop teamwork and morale.

5. To further the individual development of employees.

In recent years managers have been deluged with a flow of advice on how best to achieve these longer-run objectives. It is little wonder that they are often both bewildered and annoyed. However, there are some guidelines which they can usefully follow in making a decision.

Most research and much of the experience of recent years give a strong factual basis to the theory that a fairly high degree of subordinate-center behavior is associated with the accomplishment of the five purposes mentioned.[4] This does not mean

How to Choose a Leadership Pattern

that managers should always leave all decisions to their assistants. To provide the individual or the group with greater freedom than they are ready for at any given time may very well tend to generate anxieties and therefore inhibit rather than facilitate the attainment of desired objectives. But this should not keep managers from making a continuing effort to confront subordinates with the challenge of freedom.

In summary, there are two implications in the basic thesis that we have been developing. The first is that successful leaders are those who are keenly aware of the forces which are most relevant to their behavior at any given time. They accurately understand themselves, the individuals and groups they are dealing with, and the company and broader social environment in which they operate. And certainly they are able to assess the present readiness for growth of their subordinates.

But this sensitivity or understanding is not enough, which brings us to the second implication. Successful leaders are those who are able to behave appropriately in the light of these perceptions. If direction is in order, they are able to direct; if considerable participative freedom is called for, they are able to provide such freedom.

Thus, successful managers of people can be primarily characterized neither as strong leaders nor as permissive ones. Rather, they are people who maintain a high batting average in accurately assessing the forces that determine what their most appropriate behavior at any given time should be and in actually being able to behave accordingly. Being both insightful and flexible, they are less likely to see the problems of leadership as a dilemma.

Retrospective Commentary

Since this HBR Classic was first published in 1958, there have been many changes in organizations and in the world that have affected leadership patterns. While the article's continued popularity attests to its essential validity, we believe it can be reconsidered and updated to reflect subsequent societal changes and new management concepts.

The reasons for the article's continued relevance can be summarized briefly:

- The article contains insights and perspectives which mesh well with, and help clarify, the experiences of managers, other leaders, and students of leadership. Thus it is useful to individuals in a wide variety of organizations—industrial, governmental, educational, religious, and community.

- The concept of leadership the article defines is reflected in a continuum of leadership behavior (see Exhibit I in original article). Rather than offering a choice between two styles of leadership, democratic or authoritarian, it sanctions a range of behavior.

- The concept does not dictate to managers but helps them to analyze their own behavior. The continuum permits them to review their behavior within a context of other alternatives, without any style being labeled right or wrong.

(We have sometimes wondered if we have, perhaps, made it too easy for anyone to justify his or her style of leadership. It may be a small step between being non-judgmental and giving the impression that all behavior is equally valid and useful. The latter was not our intention. Indeed, the thrust of our endorsement was for managers who are insightful in assessing relevant forces within themselves, others, and situations, and who can be flexible in responding to these forces.)

In recognizing that our article can be updated, we are acknowledging that organizations do not exist in a vacuum but are affected by changes that occur in society. Consider, for example, the implications for organizations of these recent social developments:

- The youth revolution that expresses distrust and even contempt for organizations identified with the establishment.

- The civil rights movement that demands all minority groups be given a greater opportunity for participation and influence in the organizational processes.

How to Choose a Leadership Pattern

- The ecology and consumer movements that challenge the right of managers to make decisions without considering the interest of people outside the organization.

- The increasing national concern with the quality of working life and its relationship to worker productivity, participation, and satisfaction.

These and other societal changes make effective leadership in this decade a more challenging task, requiring even greater sensitivity and flexibility than was needed in the 1950's. Today's manager is more likely to deal with employees who resent being treated as subordinates, who may be highly critical of any organizational system, who expect to be consulted and to exert influence, and who often stand on the edge of alienation from the institution that needs their loyalty and commitment. In addition, the manager is frequently confronted by a highly turbulent, unpredictable environment.

In response to these social pressures, new concepts of management have emerged in organizations. Open-system theory, with its emphasis on subsystems' interdependency *and* on the interaction of an organization with its environment, has made a powerful impact on managers' approach to problems. Organization development has emerged as a new behavioral science approach to the improvement of individual, group, organizational, and interorganizational performance. New research has added to our understanding of motivation in the work situation. More and more executives have become concerned with social responsibility and have explored the feasibility of social audits. And a growing number of organizations, in Europe and in the United States, have conducted experiments in industrial democracy.

In light of these developments, we submit the following thoughts on how we would rewrite certain points in our original article.

The article described forces in the manager, subordinates, and the situation as givens, with the leadership pattern a result of these forces. We would now give more attention to the *interdependency* of these forces. For example, such interdependency occurs in: (a) the interplay between the manager's confidence in subordinates, their readiness to assume responsibility, and the level of group effectiveness; and (b) the impact of the behavior of the manager on that of subordinates, and vice versa.

In discussing the forces in the situation, we primarily identified organizational phenomena. We would now include forces lying outside the organization and would explore the relevant interdependencies between the organization and its environment.

In the original article, we presented the size of the rectangle in Exhibit I as a given, with its boundaries already determined by external forces—in effect, a closed system. We would now recognize the possibility of the manager and/or the subordinates taking the initiative to

How to Choose a Leadership Pattern

change those boundaries through interaction with relevant external forces—both within their own organization and in the larger society.

The article portrayed the manager as the principal and almost unilateral actor. He or she initiated and determined group functions, assumed responsibility, and exercised control. Subordinates made inputs and assumed power only at the will of the manager. Although the manager might have taken outside forces into account, it was *he* or *she* who decided where to operate on the continuum—that is, whether to announce a decision instead of trying to sell the idea to subordinates, whether to invite questions, to let subordinates decide an issue, and so on. While the manager has retained this clear prerogative in many organizations, it has been challenged in others. Even in situations where managers have retained it, however, the balance in the relationship between managers and subordinates at any given time is arrived at by interaction—direct or indirect—between the two parties.

Although power and its use by managers played a role in our article, we now realize that our concern with cooperation and collaboration, common goals, commitment, trust, and mutual caring limited our vision with respect to the realities of power. We did not attempt to deal with unions, other forms of joint worker action, or with individual workers' expressions of resistance. Today, we would recognize much more clearly the power available to *all* parties and the factors that underlie the interrelated decisions on whether to use it.

How to Choose a Leadership Pattern

In the original article, we used the terms "manager" and "subordinate." We are now uncomfortable with "subordinate" because of its demeaning, dependency-laden connotations and prefer "nonmanager." The titles "manager" and "nonmanager" make the terminological difference functional rather than hierarchical.

We assumed fairly traditional organizational structures in our original article. Now we would alter our formulation to reflect newer organizational modes which are slowly emerging, such as industrial democracy, intentional communities, and "phenomenarchy."[5] These new modes are based on observations such as the following:

- Both managers and nonmanagers may be governing forces in their group's environment, contributing to the definition of the total area of freedom.

- A group can function without a manager, with managerial functions being shared by group members.

- A group, as a unit, can be delegated authority and can assume responsibility within a larger organizational context.

Our thoughts on the question of leadership have prompted us to design a new behavior continuum (see exhibit 2) in which the total area of freedom shared by manager and nonmanagers is constantly redefined by interactions between them and the forces in the environment.

EXHIBIT 2

Continuum of manager-nonmanager behavior

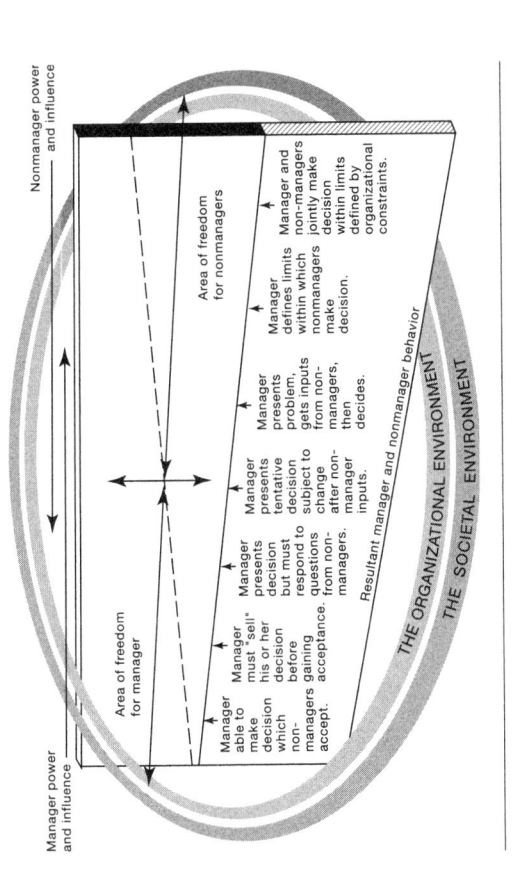

Manager power and influence
Nonmanager power and influence

Area of freedom for manager
Area of freedom for nonmanagers

Manager able to make decision which nonmanagers accept.

Manager must "sell" his or her decision before gaining acceptance.

Manager presents tentative decision subject to change after nonmanager inputs.

Manager presents decision but must respond to questions from nonmanagers.

Manager presents problem, gets inputs from nonmanagers, then decides.

Manager defines limits within which nonmanagers make decision.

Manager and non-managers jointly make decision within limits defined by organizational constraints.

Resultant manager and nonmanager behavior

THE ORGANIZATIONAL ENVIRONMENT
THE SOCIETAL ENVIRONMENT

Robert Tannenbaum and Warren H. Schmidt

The arrows in the exhibit indicate the continual flow of interdependent influence among systems and people. The points on the continuum designate the types of manager and nonmanager behavior that become possible with any given amount of freedom available to each. The new continuum is both more complex and more dynamic than the 1958 version, reflecting the organizational and societal realities of 1973.

NOTES

1. For a fuller explanation of this approach, see Leo Moore, "Too Much Management, Too Little Change," HBR January–February 1956, p. 41.

2. See also Robert Tannenbaum and Fred Massarik, "Participation by Subordinates in the

How to Choose a Leadership Pattern

Managerial Decision-Making Process," *Canadian Journal of Economics and Political Science,* August 1950, p. 413.

3. See Chris Argyris, "Top Management Dilemma: Company Needs vs. Individual Development," *Personnel,* September 1955, pp. 123–134.

4. For example, see Warren H. Schmidt and Paul C. Buchanan, *Techniques that Produce Teamwork* (New London, Arthur C. Croft Publications, 1954); and Morris S. Viteles, *Motivation and Morale in Industry* (New York, W.W. Norton & Company, Inc., 1953).

5. For a description of phenomenarchy, see Will McWhinney, "Phenomenarchy: A Suggestion for Social Redesign," *Journal of Applied Behavioral Science,* May 1973.

ABOUT THESE AUTHORS

Robert Tannenbaum was a Professor of the Development of Human Systems at the Graduate School of Management, University of California, Los Angeles at the time this article was first published.

Warren H. Schmidt is president of Chrysalis, Inc., a management training and consulting company. He is a professor emeritus at both the University of Southern California and the University of California, Los Angeles, where he was a Senior Lecturer in Behavioral Science when this article was first published.

ALSO BY THESE AUTHORS

Harvard Business Review article
"Management of Differences"